Uncomfortable
Secrets

Written by Paulina Ponce

Illustrated by Stephanie D. Halfen

Babu Books

For my children Felipe and Sofia, a constant source of joy. - *PP*

To my children, the light of my life. - *SDH*

First edition 2011

Copyright © text: Paulina Ponce
Copyright © illustrations: Stephanie D. Halfen

Design and layout: Stephanie D. Halfen

Translated by Peter Rudholm

ISBN 978-0-9831320-1-1

Do you know what the word **uncomfortable** means?

When you put on shoes that are too tight, **that's uncomfortable!**

When someone hugs you, when you **don't** want them to,
that's uncomfortable!

When your mother finds out that you lied and she looks you in the eyes and you blush, **that's uncomfortable**

What about you? Have you had an **uncomfortable** situation?
How did you feel? What did you do?

Some feel the blood rushing to their head
and their face turns red.

Some don't understand what's happening and they become pale.
Some don't say anything. What happens to you?

Use this space to draw or write what happens when you feel **uncomfortable**.

Now, let's talk about **secrets**.
Do you know what a **secret** is?

Secrets are something a friend tells you because he trusts you and asks you not to say anything to anyone. It could be where he hides his favorite candy or that he's planning a surprise party for his mom.

These kinds of **secrets** can be kept because they don't hurt anyone. They don't make anyone **uncomfortable**.

Draw a **secret** that **doesn't** make you feel **uncomfortable**.

Do you remember when we talked about certain types of hugs that make you uncomfortable? There are also hugs and kisses that we like, that make us feel good. These types of hugs we allow because they **don't make us uncomfortable**.

Anytime an adult, even one you know well,
touches you or tries to touch you in places on your
body that make you feel uncomfortable, say: **No! Stop!**
Don't keep that a secret.

It doesn't matter if the adult threatens you,
offers presents or tells you not to tell anyone.
You should tell someone that you trust.

Think of three people that you trust and draw a picture of them or write their names in the space above. Remember that a trustworthy person is someone that listens to you carefully, believes what you say and helps you solve a problem.

The secrets that are uncomfortable make you feel sad, scared or confused. **Don't keep them!**

Remember the tight shoes: they can hurt
or injure your feet. In the same way, an
uncomfortable secret can hurt your feelings.
Don't be ashamed. **Tell someone you trust!**

Sharing your worries with people you trust,
gives you the chance to work out any problem.

Try it!

Paulina Ponce, founder of Azulado, is a Child Psychologist with 17 years of experience in education and clinical psychology.
Stephanie D. Halfen is an Architect and Designer.
Together they have created this educational series as an effort to complement the hard work done by the Azulado Foundation, an Ecuadorian non-profit organization that promotes the prevention of abuse in children.

www.fundacionazulado.org

fundación
azulado
creciendo sin maltrato infantil

www.ingramcontent.com/pod-product-compliance
Lightning Source LLC
Chambersburg PA
CBHW041224040426

42443CB00002B/76